Design: Art of Design
Recipe Photography: Peter Barry
Jacket and Illustration Artwork: Jane Winton, courtesy
of Bernard Thornton Artists, London
Editors: Jillian Stewart and Kate Cranshaw

CHARTWELL BOOKS
A division of Book Sales, Inc.
POST OFFICE BOX 7100
114 Northfield Avenue
Edison, N.J. 08818-7100

CLB 3521
© 1995 CLB Publishing,
Godalming, Surrey, England.
Printed and bound in Singapore
ISBN 0-7858-0346-7

THE LITTLE BOOK ·OF·

Bread

CHARTWELL
BOOKS, INC.

Introduction

Bread, like rice, is one of the great staple foods of the world. Generally made from wheat flour of one kind or another, it comes in an infinite variety of shapes and sizes. Most of us are familiar with leavened breads – those that are made to rise by the addition of yeast, bicarbonate of soda or baking powder – fashioned into rolls, loaves and sticks. In many countries, such as Greece, Israel and India, unleavened bread is more normal, in which case the bread dough is baked in flat rounds or ovals.

Baking bread is a wonderfully rewarding craft. It is enjoyable to make, smells glorious as it bakes, and can taste far superior to commercially baked varieties. Freshly baked bread, although wonderful eaten on the day it is made, also freezes well and so is suitable for making in large quantities.

The basic process for making leavened bread involves mixing wheat flour with warm water and yeast and then kneading the dough to develop the gluten in the flour. Kneading is the rhythmic pulling and pushing of the dough until it feels sufficiently springy and elastic. The more thoroughly the dough is kneaded, the lighter the finished product will turn out. After kneading, the dough is covered and put aside to rise in a warm place. Yeast responds to warmth by producing carbon dioxide, which forms bubbles in the dough and so causes it to swell. The risen dough is then knocked back and kneaded a little more before being shaped, left to rise a second time, and then baked.

Making unleavened bread is a simpler and quicker process. The dough must still be well kneaded, but once this is achieved all that remains to be done is to roll it out into the required shape and then to cook it. Unleavened bread is not always baked. It is sometimes cooked on a very hot griddle, first on one side and then the other, like a pancake. Chapatties are Indian breads that are cooked in this way, while puris, are deep fried.

The eating of bread is a tremendously varied activity. It can be toasted, enjoyed fresh from the oven with a covering of butter, spread with peanut butter or preserves for a quick snack, or filled with countless ingredients as a delicious sandwich.

Unleavened bread is not designed to be sliced, but to be filled or wrapped around other foods. Chapatties are wonderful for wrapping up delicious mouthfuls of spicy curry.

The recipes in this book will provide a tempting introduction to bread making. Try them and you will certainly want to experiment further with the countless varieties available from around the world.

Cornbread

SERVES 9

A classic cornbread recipe. Always eat as soon as possible after baking.

PREPARATION: 15 mins
COOKING: 25-30 mins

⅔ cup yellow cornmeal
1 cup all-purpose flour
2 tbsps sugar
1 tsp salt
4 tsps baking powder
1 egg, beaten
1 cup milk
2 tbsps vegetable shortening, melted

1. Mix the cornmeal, flour, sugar, salt, and baking powder in a large bowl.

2. Make a well in the center and add the egg, milk, and melted shortening.

3. Beat very well until the ingredients are thoroughly blended.

4. Pour the mixture into a greased, square baking pan, and bake in an oven preheated to 400°F, 25-30 minutes or until risen and golden-brown on top.

5. As a variation, add 2 tbsps shredded American cheese. Cut into squares to serve.

Boston Brown Bread

MAKES 1 LARGE LOAF OR 4-6 SMALL LOAVES

This is a very different kind of bread, as it is cooked in a tin can. Try adding chopped raisins, dates, or prunes to the mixture.

PREPARATION: 20 mins
COOKING: 3-4 hrs

2 cups fine cornmeal
2 cups wholewheat flour
1 cup all-purpose flour
Pinch salt
6 tbsps molasses mixed with 1 tsp baking soda
2 cups cold water
Butter or oil
Boiling water

1. Sift the dry ingredients into a large bowl and return the bran to the bowl.

2. Mix the molasses, baking soda and water together. Make a well in the center of the flour, and pour in the mixture. Mix just until well blended.

Step 3 Fill the cans with the bread mixture to about two thirds full.

Step 4 Cover the tops of the cans tightly with foil and place on a rack in boiling water to come halfway up the sides.

3. Use a large can from canned tomatoes, coffee, or canned fruit, or alternatively, use 4-6 smaller cans. Wash them well and remove the labels, then grease generously. Spoon the bread mixture to come about two-thirds of the way up the sides of the cans. Cover the tops of the cans lightly with greased foil and secure with string.

4. Stand them on a rack in a deep saucepan. Pour enough boiling water around the cans to come about halfway up their sides. Allow the water to bubble gently, and steam the bread 3-4 hours in the covered pan.

5. Add more boiling water as necessary during cooking. The bread is cooked when a cocktail stick inserted into the center of the bread comes out clean. Serve warm with butter or cream cheese.

Naan Bread

Although naans are traditionally cooked in a Tandoor, a very hot oven will work well, but the distinctive taste of clay cooking will be missing.

PREPARATION: 10-15 mins, plus ¾-1¼ hrs rising time
COOKING: 20-25 mins

---

4 cups all-purpose flour
1 tsp salt
1 tsp black onion seeds (optional)
1 tsp sugar
1½ envelopes yeast
⅔ cup plain yogurt
½ cup lukewarm milk
1 medium egg, beaten
½ cup ghee or butter, melted
2 tbsps sesame seeds or white poppyseeds

---

1. Put the flour, salt, black onion seeds, sugar, and yeast into a large bowl and mix well. Reserve 1 tbsp yogurt, and add the rest to the milk, and blend thoroughly.

2. Add the milk-and-yogurt mixture, egg, and ghee to the flour. Knead with your hands or in a food processor until à soft and springy dough is formed.

3. Place the dough in a large oiled plastic food bag. Tie the bag at the top so that the dough has plenty of room to expand.

4. Rinse a metal bowl with hot water and put the bag of dough in it. Put the bowl in a warm place for ½-1 hour, or until the dough has doubled in size. Do not allow the dough to become too warm as this will kill the yeast.

5. Divide the dough into 8 balls, cover them, and keep aside for 10-15 minutes.

6. Preheat an oven to 450°F and put in an ungreased baking tray to heat about 10 minutes. Remove the baking tray from the oven and line with greased parchment paper or nonstick baking paper.

7. Take one of the balls and stretch it gently with both hands to make a teardrop shape. Lay this on the baking tray and press it gently to stretch it to about 6-7 inches in length, maintaining the teardrop shape. Shape 2-3 at a time and brush with some of the reserved yogurt, then sprinkle with some of the seeds. Bake at the top of the oven 10-12 minutes, or until puffed and browned.

Quick Home-Made Bread

MAKES 3 LOAVES

The molasses in this recipe gives the bread an attractive appearance.

PREPARATION: 20 mins
COOKING: 35-40 mins

---

1 tbsp molasses
1 tbsp sunflower oil
2½ cups hand-hot water
13 cups 100% wholewheat flour
2 envelopes active dry yeast
3 tsps sea salt

---

1. Oil three 2-quart bread pans and set aside in a warm place.

2. Add the molasses and oil to half the water, mix and set aside.

3. Place the flour, yeast, and salt into a large bowl and mix together thoroughly.

4. Gradually pour the water and molasses mixture into the flour, mixing in with your hands.

5. Add the remaining water gradually until the dough is wetted but not sticky. You may not require all the water.

6. Knead the dough about a dozen times, divide the dough between the three pans, and press down firmly. Cover with a damp cloth.

7. Leave to rise in a warm place 5-10 minutes or until the dough has risen near to the top of the pans.

8. Bake in an oven preheated to 425°F, 35-40 minutes, or until the loaves sound hollow when tapped underneath.

Puris

The dough for this bread can be made in advance, but they should be rolled out and fried just prior to serving.

PREPARATION: 5-10 mins
COOKING: 15-20 mins

2½ cups fine wholewheat flour
½ tsp salt
¼ tsp sugar
1 tbsp margarine
About 1 cup warm water (quantity will depend on the texture of the flour)
Oil for deep-frying

---

1. In a bowl, mix the flour, salt, and sugar. Rub in the margarine. Now slowly add enough of the water, mixing and kneading, to form a stiff dough.

2. Divide the dough into 14-15 equal portions, and roll into balls about 1½ inches in diameter. Dust each lightly with a little extra flour, and flatten into round cakes. Cover them with a damp cloth.

3. Roll out the puris to 3½-inch diameter disks. Rolling out should be done evenly to ensure tight edges, which help the puris to puff up when they are cooked. If they are damaged or pierced they will not puff up.

4. It is easier to roll and fry one puri at a time. Do not stack them on top of each other as they will all stick together.

5. Heat the oil to 325°F in a deep-fat fryer. Place one puri at a time in the oil, and gently press it down with a slotted spoon. As soon as the puri puffs up, turn it over and cook about 30 seconds. Drain on kitchen paper. Fry the remaining puris in the same way.

6. Do not heap the fried puris one on top of the other, but place them on an open tray so as not to flatten or damage them.

Scofa Bread

MAKES 1 LOAF

This chunky bread is ideal served warm with a ploughman's lunch or a salad.

PREPARATION: 10 mins
COOKING: 1 hr

5 cups self-rising wholewheat flour
2 cups bran
1 tsp salt
½ cup butter or margarine
Just under 2¼ cups water
1 tbsp oil

1. Put the flour, bran, and salt into a mixing bowl.

2. Rub in the butter and mix the water and oil together.

3. Make a well in the center of the flour and pour in the water and oil.

4. Mix in the flour, gradually drawing it into the liquid mixture from the sides, until a dough is formed.

5. Shape into a 7-inch round and place on a greased baking tray.

6. With a sharp knife, mark into four sections cutting to within ½ inch of the bottom.

7. Bake just above the center of an oven preheated to 400°F, about 1 hour or until nicely browned and hollow-sounding when tapped underneath.

8. Remove from the oven and wrap in a clean cloth to cool.

Rotis

MAKES 8 Rotis

Rotis are a type of Indian unleavened wholewheat bread. If you cannot get special chapatti flour, use equal quantities of wholewheat and all-purpose flour.

PREPARATION: 20-25 mins
COOKING: 25-30 mins

½ tsp salt
4 tbsps butter, or ghee
½ cups each wholewheat and all-purpose flour
About 1 cup warm water (quantity depends on the texture of the flour)
2 tbsps ghee or unsalted butter, for frying

---

1. Rub the salt and fat into the flour until it resembles coarse breadcrumbs.

2. Gradually add the water and knead until a soft and pliable dough is formed. This may be done in a food processor, if wished.

3. Divide the dough into 8 round balls. Flatten each between your palms into a round cake and dust it very lightly in a little all-purpose flour.

4. Roll them out to circles about 6 inches in diameter. Cover the rest of the dough with a damp cloth while you are working.

5. Heat a heavy-based skillet over a medium heat. When the pan is hot, place a roti on it, and flip it over after about 30 seconds. Spread 1 tsp ghee or butter over it and turn the roti over.

6. Repeat the process for the other side. Brown both sides evenly and remove from heat. Repeat with the remaining rotis.

7. To keep the rotis warm, line a piece of foil with kitchen paper, and put the cooked rotis on one half. Cover with the other half and seal the edges. This will keep them warm for 30-40 minutes.

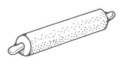

Soft Bread Cakes

MAKES 6

The bread cakes may be split and toasted, buttered, and then filled with cheese, or bacon and fried eggs.

PREPARATION: 30 mins
COOKING: 15 mins

3 cups wholewheat flour
1 tsp salt
2 tbsps fresh yeast
1 tsp brown sugar
¾ cup milk
2 tbsps vegetable fat
1 egg, beaten

1. Put the flour and salt in a mixing bowl.

2. Cream the yeast and sugar together until smooth.

3. Warm the milk with the vegetable fat.

4. Mix the milk and fat with the creamed yeast, and stir in the beaten egg.

5. Make a well in the flour and work the milk mixture in gradually to make a soft dough.

6. Knead lightly then form into six round cakes.

7. Cover and leave to rise for 20 minutes in a warm place.

8. Bake in an oven preheated to 425°F, about 15 minutes.

9. Glaze with beaten egg – or milk and sugar – a few minutes before removing from the oven.

Golden Raisin Soda Bread

SERVES 6-8

Golden raisins add a natural sweetness that makes this bread ideal for serving as a tea-time treat.

PREPARATION: 15 mins
COOKING: 35 mins

4 cups all-purpose flour
1 tsp salt
1 tsp baking soda
1 tsp cream of tartar
4 tbsps golden raisins
1¼ cups milk mixed with 1 tbsp plain yogurt

1. Sift together the flour, salt, baking soda, and cream of tartar into a mixing bowl.

2. Add the golden raisins and mix into the flour quickly, making a slight well in the center of the flour as you do so.

3. Pour the milk into the well in the flour, and mix with a round-bladed knife to form a firm dough, but not too stiff that is.

Step 6 Cut a deep cross into the top of the bread dough, using a sharp knife.

Step 8 Turn the loaf upside down on the baking tray, before returning to the oven for a further 10 minutes.

4. Turn the dough onto a lightly-floured board, and knead quickly to bring all the ingredients together well.

5. Shape the dough into a round, and flatten it slightly with the palm of your hand.

6. Place the dough round on a lightly-greased and floured baking tray. Cut a deep cross into the top of the dough with a sharp knife.

7. Bake the dough in an oven preheated to 400°F, 25 minutes.

8. After this time, turn the loaf upside-down on the tray and return to the oven a further 10 minutes to dry out completely.

9. Wrap the baked loaf in a damp cloth and place on a wire rack to cool completely.

Parathas

MAKES 4

A paratha is a crisp, rich unleavened bread. It is rather like making flaky pastry but the method is simpler.

PREPARATION: 30 mins
COOKING: 20 mins

---

3 cups wholewheat flour plus 1 tbsp extra flour
   for dusting
½ tsp salt
⅔ cup ghee or unsalted butter
½ cup warm water

---

1. Sift the flour and the salt together then rub in 4 tbsps of the ghee until thoroughly mixed.

2. Gradually add the water, and knead to a soft and pliable dough.

3. Divide the dough into 4 equal-sized balls and flatten them between your palms.

4. Dust each with the extra flour and roll out to 8-inch circles. Spread about 1 tsp of the remaining ghee evenly on each.

5. Roll up each circle until you have tubes about 1 inch wide and 8 inches long. Gently stretch the dough lengthwise and then curl the ends inwards in an anti-clockwise direction to resemble backward S's.

6. Now flip the upper halves of each onto the lower halves and flatten. Lightly dust them all over with flour and roll out again until the dough is about 8 inches in diameter and ⅛ inch in thickness.

7. Melt the reamining ghee and reserve it. Heat a skillet, preferably a cast iron one, over a medium heat and place one paratha on it. Flip it over after about 30 seconds.

8. Spread with 1 tbsp of the melted ghee and flip it over again. Lower the heat, and spread 1 tbsp of the melted ghee on this side as well.

9. Press the paratha gently into the pan, using a metal spatula. Flip it over after 1 minute, and repeat the pressing action. Cook the second side 1 minute.

10. Continue to cook both sides evenly until the paratha is uniformly light brown. Cook the remaining parathas in the same way.

Wholewheat Bread

MAKES 2 LOAVES

This very moist bread, which uses no yeast, will last for days. If wished add some caraway seeds to the dough before baking and sprinkle some on top of the loaves to decorate.

PREPARATION: 20 mins
COOKING: 1¼-1½hrs

6 cups wholewheat flour
1 cup all-purpose flour
¾ cup raw oatmeal
4 tbsps bran
1½ cups pinhead or coarse, raw oatmeal
4 tbsps wheatgerm
½ tsp baking powder
½ tsp sea salt
2 eggs, beaten
5 cups milk

1. Mix all the dry ingredients together in a large bowl, and make a well in the center.

2. Add the eggs and milk to the well in the dry ingredients, and gradually incorporate the dry ingredients into the liquid until the mixture is blended.

3. Spoon into 2 greased one-quart loaf pans and bake in the center of an oven preheated to 350°F, 1¼-1½ hours. When baked, the loaves should sound hollow when tapped underneath.

4. Turn out of the pans to cool on a wire rack.

Tandoori Rotis

MAKES 8

Tandoori Rotis are breads from India, which are traditionally cooked in the Tandoor – a barrel-shaped clay oven that distributes an even and fierce heat. However, they can be cooked in a very hot conventional oven, and taste equally delicious though the flavor will be a little different.

PREPARATION: 10-15 mins, plus 30-45 mins rising time

COOKING: 25 mins

⅔ cup plain yogurt
4 cups all-purpose flour
1 tsp sugar
1 tsp baking powder
½ tsp salt
1½ envelopes quick-acting dry yeast
1 tbsp ghee or unsalted butter
1 medium egg, beaten
⅔ cup warm milk

---

1. Beat the yogurt until smooth, and set aside.

2. In a large bowl, sift the flour with the sugar, baking powder, salt, and yeast. Add the ghee and mix thoroughly. Add the yogurt and egg and knead well. Use food processor for mixing and kneading, if preferred.

3. Gradually add the warm milk and keep kneading until a smooth and springy dough is formed.

4. Place the dough in a large, oiled plastic food bag. Tie the bag closed leaving plenty of room for the dough to expand.

5. Rinse a large metal bowl with hot water and put the bag of dough in it. Place the bowl in a warm place for ½-¾ hour or until almost doubled in volume.

6. Line a baking tray with greased nonstick baking paper.

7. Divide the dough into 8 equal-sized balls, then flatten them.

8. Dust lightly with a little flour and gently roll them out to 4-inch disks. Place on the prepared baking tray.

9. Bake in an oven preheated to 450°F 10-12 minutes. Turn the rotis over and bake a further 2 minutes.

Crisp Wholegrain Rolls

MAKES 10

For a crisp crust brush the rolls with salted water and sprinkle with cracked wheat before baking. Use any combination of wholegrain flours with a preponderance of wholewheat flour for easy rising.

PREPARATION: 1 hr
COOKING: 15-20 mins

---

3 cups wholegrain flour
1 tsp salt
1 tbsp fresh yeast or 2 tsps dry yeast
1 tsp brown sugar
1 cup warm water
2 tbsps vegetable fat, melted

---

1. Place the flour and salt in a mixing bowl and leave in a warm place.

2. Cream the yeast and sugar together with three-quarters of the warm water.

3. Make a well in the middle of the flour and pour in the yeast mixture.

4. Add the melted fat and mix to a pliable dough, adding the remaining water as necessary.

5. Knead lightly for a minute or two, then cover with a clean damp cloth and leave in a warm place until the dough has doubled in size.

6. Knead again 3-5 minutes and shape into 10 smooth rolls.

7. Place well apart on a floured baking tray, cover, and leave in a warm place until the rolls have doubled in size.

8. Bake in the center of an oven preheated to 425°F, 15-20 minutes, or until the rolls sound hollow when tapped underneath. Cool on a wire rack.

Batura

SERVES 6

Batura is a yeast-risen bread that is made of flour and then deep-fried. The dough is moistened with plain yogurt and has a soft, velvet-like texture.

PREPARATION: 5-10 mins, plus 45 mins rising
COOKING: 12-15 mins

3 cups all-purpose flour
1 tsp salt
2 tsps fast-acting or dry yeast
1 egg, beaten
⅔ cup plain yogurt
2-3 tbsps warm water
Oil for deep-frying

1. Put the flour, salt, and yeast in a bowl and mix well. Add the egg, yogurt, and water and knead until a soft and pliable dough is formed. Use a food processor if wished.

2. Put the dough in a large oiled plastic bag. Tie the bag at the top, leaving plenty of room for the dough to expand.

3. Put the bag into a metal bowl or saucepan which has been rinsed out in hot water, and leave in a warm place for 45 minutes to rise.

4. Remove the dough from the bag and divide it into 6 equal portions. Roll each into a ball then flatten into round cakes.

5. Dust one cake lightly in a little flour and roll out gently to a circle of about 6 inches in diameter.

6. Heat the oil to 350°F in a deep-fat fryer. Place one batura in the hot oil and fry it 1 minute; turn it over and fry the other side for a further minute, or until it is a rich creamy color. Drain on kitchen paper.

7. Make and fry all the baturas the same way. It is easier to roll out and fry one batura at a time rather than rolling them all out first.

Rich Stollen Bread

MAKES 1 LOAF

This makes an attractive centerpiece for a Christmas feast.

PREPARATION: 25 mins plus 1¾ hrs proving
COOKING: 30 mins

1¼ cups unbleached all-purpose flour
Pinch salt
1 tbsp fresh yeast
1 tbsp light brown sugar
½ cup milk, warmed
1 egg, beaten

Filling
1 egg
1 cup ground almonds
4 tbsps poppyseeds, plus extra for decoration
4 tbsps raisins, soaked overnight
4 tbsps currants
4 tbsps candied cherries, chopped
4 tbsps light brown sugar, finely ground in a
    blender
2 tbsps dates, chopped
Juice of ½ lemon
Almond extract, to taste

2 tbsps butter
1 egg, beaten, to glaze
Flaked almonds

---

1. Place the flour and salt in a bowl. Cream the yeast and sugar together, add the milk, and stir well. Add the beaten egg, and leave for a few minutes in a warm place.

2. Add the mixture to the flour and mix. Knead well 5 minutes. Put into a clean bowl, cover, and leave in a warm place 40 minutes.

3. To make the filling, beat the egg, reserving a little, and add all the other filling ingredients. Mix well – the mixture should be fairly moist.

4. To assemble, knock back the dough, and roll out to a rectangle 12 × 8 inches.

5. Working with a short end towards you, dot half the butter over the top two-thirds of the dough. Fold the bottom third up, then fold down the top to cover. Seal the edges, and make a one quarter turn.

6. Roll out to a rectangle shape again, and repeat with the remainder of the butter. Fold over as before, but do not roll out. Cover and chill for ½ hour, then roll out as before.

7. Cover with the filling, leaving a tiny margin around the edges. Roll from a short side and tuck in the ends. Place on a baking tray and brush with the beaten egg.

8. Mark out in 1-inch slices, snipping either side with scissors. Cover with some flaked almonds and poppyseeds and leave to prove for a further 15 minutes. Bake in an oven preheated to 400°F, 30 minutes.

Chapatties

MAKES 14

A chapatti is a dry-roasted, unleavened bread best eaten as soon as it is cooked. They are not as filling as Rotis or Parathas, so allow about 2-3 chapatties per person.

PREPARATION: 20-25 mins, plus ½-1 hr proving
COOKING: 35-40 mins

---

3 cups fine wholewheat flour
½ tsp salt
1 tbsp butter, or ghee
About 1 cup warm water (quantity depends on the texture of the flour)
1 tbsp extra flour in a shallow bowl or plate

---

1. Put the flour and salt in a large bowl, and rub in the fat. Gradually add the water, and keep mixing and kneading until a soft and pliable dough is formed.

2. Lightly oil the bowl, add the dough, and cover with a damp cloth. Leave to stand ½-1 hour in a warm place.

3. Divide the dough into 14 pieces, and roll into balls. Flatten the balls to make round cakes, then dip each into the extra flour, and roll out into disks about 6 inches in diameter.

4. Heat an iron griddle or heavy-based skillet over a medium heat and place a chapatti on it. Cook 30 seconds then turn the chapatti over.

5. Cook until brown spots appear on both sides, turning frequently. Do not over-heat the griddle or skillet or the chapatties will stick and start to burn.

6. To keep the chapatties warm, line a piece of foil with kitchen paper, and place the chapatties on one end. Cover with the other end and seal the edges.

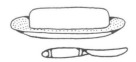

Chocolate Cinnamon Sweet Bread

MAKES 1 LOAF

Pull this bread apart to serve in individual pieces rather than slicing it. For a savory version, use Parmesan and herbs instead of sugar and spice.

PREPARATION: 2 hrs, including rising
COOKING: 45-50 mins

Dough
½ cup sugar
1 envelope dried yeast
4 tbsps warm water
3-3½ cups all-purpose flour
5 tbsps butter, softened
5 eggs

Topping
1 cup sugar
2 tsps each cinnamon and cocoa powder
6 tbsps finely-chopped nuts
½ cup melted butter

1. Add the yeast and 1 tbsp of the sugar to the water. Leave in a warm place until foaming.

2. Sift 3 cups of the flour into a bowl, add the sugar and a pinch of salt. Rub in the butter.

3. Add 2 of the eggs and the yeast mixture, mixing in well. Add the remaining eggs one at a time until the mixture forms a soft, spongy dough. Add the remaining flour as necessary. Knead 10 minutes on a lightly-floured surface

Step 5 Roll the dough in melted butter and then in the sugar mixture.

until smooth and elastic.

4. Place the dough in a greased bowl, cover loosely, and put in a warm place 1-1½ hours, or until doubled in bulk.

5. Knock the dough down and knead it again for about 5 minutes. Shape into 2-inch balls. Mix the topping ingredients together, except for the melted butter. Roll the dough in the butter, and then the sugar.

6. Layer up the dough balls in a well-greased tube pan. Cover and allow to rise again about 15 minutes. Bake in an oven preheated to 350°F, about 45-50 minutes. Loosen from the pan and unmold.

Loochis

MAKES 14-15 Loochis

These Indian breads are similar to puris – the main difference is that they are made with all-purpose flour instead of wholewheat flour.

PREPARATION: 10-15 mins
COOKING: 15-20 mins

2½ cups all-purpose flour plus 1 tbsp extra flour
   for dusting
½ tsp salt
¼ tsp sugar
1 tsp black onion seeds (optional)
1 tbsp butter or ghee
About 1 cup warm water (this will depend on
   the texture of the flour)
Oil for deep-frying

---

1. In a large bowl, mix the flour, salt, sugar, and black onion seeds. Rub in the fat and gradually add the water. Knead until a stiff dough is formed.

2. Divide the dough into 14-15 walnut-sized balls. Press them down gently to make flat, ½-inch-thick round cakes. Cover with a damp cloth.

3. Dust each flattened cake lightly with extra flour, and roll out to about 3½-inch disks. It is easier to roll out and fry one Loochi at a time unless you have someone to help you. If you roll out all of them first, keep in a single layer – otherwise they may stick together.

4. To ensure that the Loochis puff up during cooking, roll them out carefully and evenly, without damaging or piercing them.

5. Heat the oil to 325°F in a deep-fat fryer. Place one Loochi at a time in the hot oil – it will soon float to the surface and start puffing up. Use a flat, slotted spoon to press it down gently on the edge to help it cook evenly. As soon as the Loochi puffs up, turn it over gently, and cook about 30 seconds or until lightly-browned. Drain on kitchen paper. Fry the rest of the Loochis the same way.

6. Keep the fried Loochis warm in a hot oven. Spread them out in a single layer so they don't get damaged.

Index